How To Generate Leads Using LinkedIn

AJ - Ashley Johnson

AJ - Ashley Johnson

Copyright © 2018 AJ - Ashley Johnson

All rights reserved.

DEDICATION

To the coaches, mentors, peers, leaders, *and bosses* that led me to where I am today.

CONTENTS

	ACKNOWLEDGMENTS	i
1	MOTIVATING THE TEAMS	1
2	LINKEDIN SALES NAVIGATOR	24
3	SOCIAL SELLING	34
4	LINKEDIN DATA	42
5	AUTOMATION	45
6	WILL IT WORK FOR YOU?	53
7	ABOUT THE AUTHOR	60

How To Generate Leads Using LinkedIn

ACKNOWLEDGMENTS

I thank my Vistage group and the wonderful network that Vistage has provided to me for offering many tips to help me improve this process and empower me as a marketing leader. Ken Proctor, Bob Wells, Jennifer Devine, Lorie Clements, Owais Qureshi, Lanie Vanek, Rob Thompson, Michael Kuchar, Stephen Johnson, Dan Geddes, and Jess Bailey - I appreciate your honesty and inspiration.

Gina Maurino and Julie Webie, thank you for encouraging me to publish this book. I hope this step-by-step guide helps entrepreneurs, sales professionals, marketers, and anyone else looking to broaden their network using LinkedIn.

How To Generate Leads Using LinkedIn

WHY LINKEDIN?

Contrary to what many of the LinkedIn-savvy believe, there is still a rather large population of our workforce that isn't taking advantage of LinkedIn. Why is that? We see fewer blue collar workers. We see fewer women. In general, the network is predominantly used by white-collar professionals. Many of these professionals still mistakenly believe that

LinkedIn's sole purpose is for recruiting and finding work, but that is just one of many powerful tools that LinkedIn offers to both professionals and to organizations.

Whether you are the owner of the business or a successful salesperson or marketer - the burden of driving business rests on your shoulders and the ways in which you can promote your business seem endless. A constant change in technology, and the only consistent quality that the social platforms possess are their knack for reinventing their dashboards making it seem impossible to keep up with let alone train a staff on.

Why then do I recommend LinkedIn to generate leads for your business? It isn't for the simplicity. It is simply because it works and has been tried and tested in nearly every B2B setting.

Not only does this process work tremendously well for B2B sales, but this process can be managed internally by your existing teams allowing you to use your remaining marketing budget on longer-term strategies.

I hope readers are inspired to create a unique LinkedIn strategy for their business to meet their business objectives.

MOTIVATING THE TEAMS

Whether you are the leader of the team rolling out this new lead generation strategy or you are a sales rep looking to increase the productivity of the team, there are many motivating factors to get buy-in from the entire team.

Motivation

When corporate rolls out initiatives it takes time, patience, and a lot of communication to get the teams on board. Guiding your teams on how to implement LinkedIn Lead Generation directly benefits them in multiple ways which will be critical for you to communicate this early on to encourage team buy-in. Below are a few of the most common "Why" examples that we use to motivate teams.

Motivation for Executives:

+ Notoriety, positioning the executives to attract industry and media attention in addition to boosting their credibility as an industry thought-leader.

+ Conference Speaking, leadership team will have a reputable profile to encourage conference panel/session/keynote opportunities

+ Business Development, for leadership that participates in establishing relationships with large corporate accounts. The process increases connectivity to ideal accounts.

Motivation for Sales:

- + More sales = more money.
- + Industry acknowledgment and attention.
- + Optimizes coordination with marketing.

Motivation for Marketing:

- + More sales = more marketing budget for special projects.
- + Industry acknowledgment and attention.
- + Improves communication with the sales team.

Consistency

Whether you are a team of two or a team of 10,000, keeping the team consistent on message can be a constant struggle. Your teams are often asked, "What do you do?" which is typically followed with, "What does your company do?" and this is when things should be consistent.

Here are just a few tips to improve message consistency:

- + Have a clear company mission. Make this mission available on your corporate website, add this to all internal communications, and include it in any internal handbooks. A clear mission is one sentence long.

- + Have an elevator pitch for all staff, not just sales. Often we find that only sales and marketing teams actually know or have a company elevator pitch, but your brand's army extends much greater than simply sales and marketing staff.

- + Have an engaging employee handbook. Honestly, no one wants to read a boring handbook, but making it more visual or animated digitally will encourage more employees to take the time to learn the valuable content that you have to share.

Most of us know that consistency of message reaches beyond what we might say in conversation. Consistency should cover your team's LinkedIn profiles. I recommend pushing this to the entire staff, but it is critical for any client-facing personnel to get on board and make a cohesive impression on the public.

Personal Cover Photo

I urge your marketing advisor to oversee the design of an appropriately sized and tested LinkedIn cover photo for personal profile use. I recommend the use of company branded cover photos be required for any client-facing team members and strongly encouraged for all other supporting staff.

Should you create multiple branded cover photos? If you are a larger organization with multiple revenue streams, then I encourage the design of multiple cover photos to be used on the appropriate personal employee and showcase profiles.

Different people within your organization are going to appear within different search results. Think specifically about how your customers talk about your business. Does the textual and visual content of your cover photo describe what you do for your customers? Is there a way to intrigue them enough to either do business with you or refer business to you just by simply viewing your profile cover photo? Give this some considerable thought.

My tips for hitting the mark on cover photo design:

- + Use limited text. I recommend sticking with the billboard rule and limiting the text to less than six words.

- + Make it eye-catching! Much of what we see on LinkedIn is white, blue, and boring. Don't be like those guys. Stand out from the rest.

- + Don't be obnoxiously salesy. Be bold, but not pushy.

- + Don't overthink the text. Forget everything that you know about your business and think about the impression that this would give to someone in your target audience, that has never heard anything about you before.

- + Going to circle back around and stress the importance of not cramming a ton of text on here. To be frank, most people don't care to read a paragraph of text on a graphic and your goal here is simply to catch their eye.

{ Having trouble communicating the importance of limiting text in a design piece? }

I recommend letting the visual elements speak for itself. It is science, humans process visual data better. Our brains process images 60,000 times faster than text. More visual content = more sales. It is science, boss.

Personal Profile Photo

All members of the client-facing staff should have headshots as their profile photos. Logos and other photos not of the person's face should be discouraged as it decreases their credibility. Headshots should have good lighting and a clean appearance. Headshots can be interesting and if you have a corporate brand persona, then encourage your staff to emulate that persona in their photos.

Personal Headline

The LinkedIn headline gets a lot of attention from marketers because of its power. Your headline, name and profile picture all end up in the email inbox of anybody that you request to connect with which makes it ultra important to get right. Like the cover photo, I recommend creating at least three different headlines for staff to utilize. You may even create a template for staff in the form of an ad lib which would allow specialized personnel to really showcase their own unique value add.

Headline tips:

+ In one short sentence, explain who you are professionally.

+ Don't leave your headline on the default job title.

+ Use terms that you want to be most associated with in the search results, this is especially important for those interested in personal brand growth.

+ If the ideal person landed on your page, then what action would you want them to take? The answer to this may be used as inspiration.

+ Consider adding a phone number or another way to reach you.

Personal Summary

Your LinkedIn summary is important for a few reasons, but in my personal opinion the most important reason: Whatever content you put in this section is content that you will be ranked for in the search results... in other words, this area can get you some really good (and free) SEO.

My poor man's guide to SEO is to think about who it is that you would want to find your profile. Then think about all of the terms and ways that they might try to search for you... generally they are going to use slightly different terms than you might ordinarily think to use to describe yourself.

Your summary should do just that: summarize your experience and your current functions. This is not the place to sell your company, but your summary can sell your company if written properly. Talk about you and your role within your current company and how you have been able to impact the overall mission of your company. The message will be stronger than a sales pitch summary.

Company Information

There are endless ways to use your corporate profile on LinkedIn, but when the profile itself isn't very strong then those efforts often go to waste. The following are ways that can you boost your credibility within LinkedIn and help aid the efforts of your sales teams.

- Use a .PNG file of your logo as the profile photo. Your .png version of your logo should have a transparent background which will be important when your company appears on your employees profile pages.

- Add a cover photo. The dimensions of this photo can be tricky to get just right as the recommended size still typically cuts off portions of the image, but the right graphic designer can adjust this for you.

- Custom overview. This is not the section for copying what is already on your corporate website and pasting it over to LinkedIn. This is the opportunity to be authentic, talk about what makes doing business with your company special. Talk about what makes working with your company special. This page can be used as a sales and recruiting tool.

- Use content inbox for corporate content if you do not already maintain a blog regularly and use that content as updates to your corporate network.

- Advise employees and stakeholders to share / engage in corporate content that is shared via LinkedIn.

Editing Corporate Pages

Step 1. Login to LinkedIn from the personal account(s) that are listed as administrators of the main company page. If you are unsure of who the admin is on your account, then open a ticket with LinkedIn and they will allow you to take over as long as you have an email account that matches the domain listed for the company.

Step 2. Head over to the company page once logged in to the appropriate account and it should look like this:

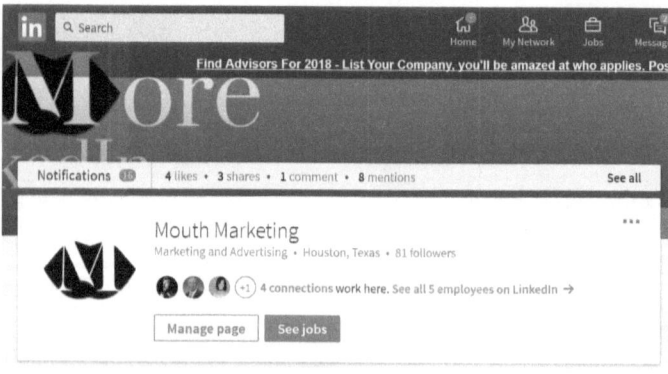

Step 3. On this page you will click "Manage

page"

Step 4. You will be taken to a page that looks like the below image, but you want to click the "Overview" tab at the top. This page can be a little confusing if you haven't edited your corporate page in a while... Things move around a lot!

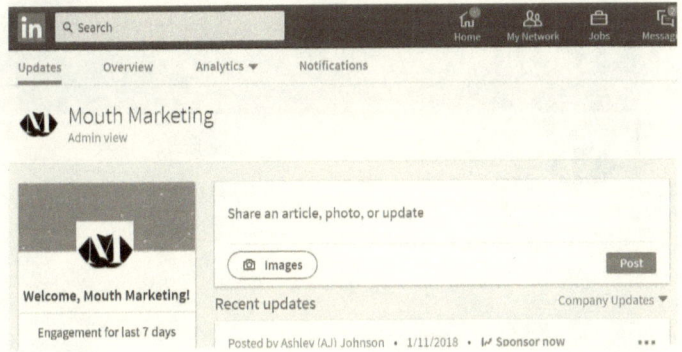

Step 5. Once on the overview page, this is where you will be able to make all of those important changes and updates. This page will look a lot like this:

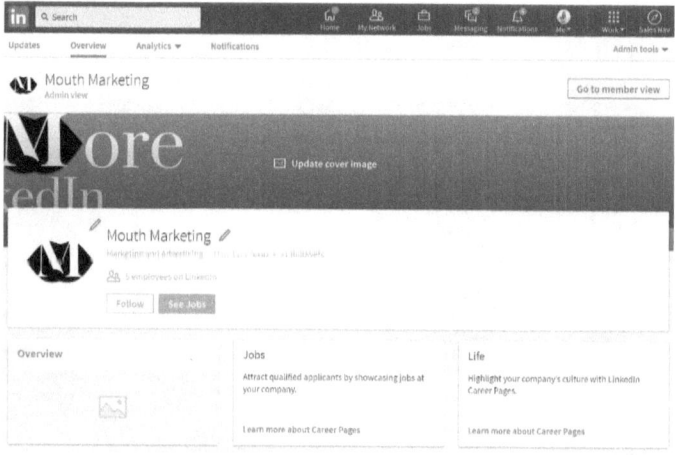

LINKEDIN SALES NAVIGATOR

How to Upgrade

Before we get into the powers of LinkedIn Sales Navigator, lets first get you upgraded to premium if you aren't already there...

Step 1. Your home page should look something like this, but LinkedIn also doesn't make navigating home pages very simple as not everyone's home page looks the same. If your page does not look like the one below, then contact your friends at Mouth Marketing.

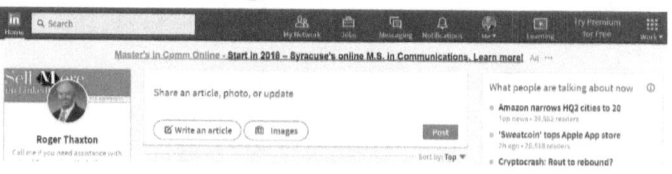

Step 2. Click "Try Premium for Free" on the top right of the menu bar. Once clicked, you will land on this page:

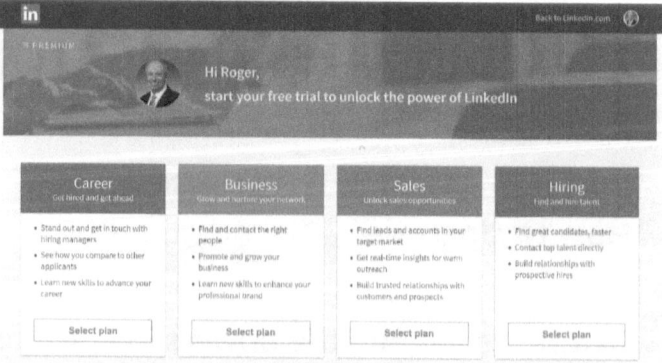

Step 3. To access the correct premium upgrade, click the "Select plan" button underneath the Sales column. In the past, the features fell under other plans, but LinkedIn has made a series of feature adjustments so the plan that you need for this next section is the Sales plan.

Setting up Sales Navigator

Step 1. Once you complete the upgrade, you will arrive at a page that looks like the below image. Click continue.

Step 2. The next series of pages will be helpful for your Sales Navigator newsfeed. Note: The Sales Navigator newsfeed is different than the newsfeed that you see on the homepage of your regular LinkedIn account. Sales Navigator will always open in a separate window.

Tips for these settings:

+ First, start by asking yourself: Who are your target customers as they appear on LinkedIn? Who are you trying to get in front of? Where are these people located? How far do you want to try to reach your target audience? Fine-tune this section so that LinkedIn can display any relevant updates from those people.

+ Industry: You may be industry specific, think about what industries you prefer to do business. LinkedIn also labels industries differently than you may immediately think about so now is the ideal time to browse through their comprehensive list and make your selections.

+ Company Size: This can be a great indicator of budgets. If you prefer to work with smaller companies, then you can certainly target the smaller businesses. If you prefer to work with medium sized businesses or large corporations, then now would be the time to make those appropriate selections. Please contact your friends at Mouth Marketing if you have questions about how to determine the appropriate target for company size or any of the filter options.

- + Function: This is my personal favorite filter option because LinkedIn is smart enough to know what employees in each company are managing. If you target specific job titles, rather than searching always by job title - search by job function and you will find a list of your ideal client with variations of the same job title or sometimes very odd job titles.

- + Seniority Level: We want to target the decision makers and the influencers. Select all of the typical seniority levels responsible for approving business with your organization.

Step 3. This page trips up a lot of new Navigator users, but it is actually a rather powerful feature. I suggest that you enter in companies that you would really like to do business with, companies that you are currently doing business with, and companies that you did business with in the past. You will be updated on important changes within these companies which can be a key indicator on when to reach out to these accounts.

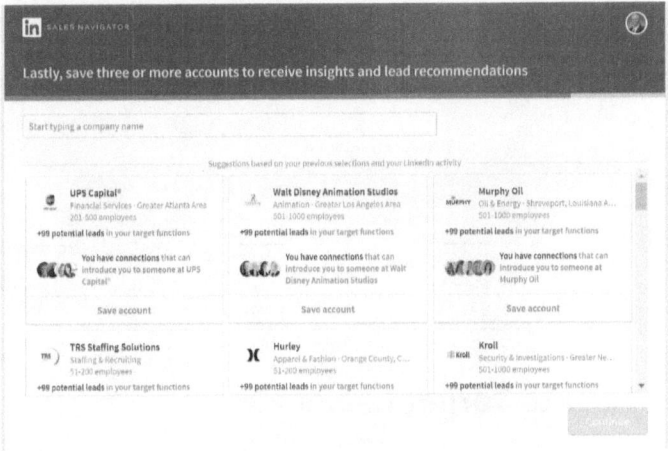

Step 4. That's it! You are ready to start searching for leads.

How to Target Leads

The next section is key in building up your database and social reach on LinkedIn.

Step 1. To get back into the Sales Navigator dashboard from LinkedIn you will want to login to LinkedIn as usual from a desktop or laptop, then click "Sales Nav" at the top right in the menu bar.

Step 2. A separate window or tab will open with your Sales Navigator dashboard. It should look something like the below image. The dashboard will show you information about your saved leads (will talk about this in a bit) and saved accounts.

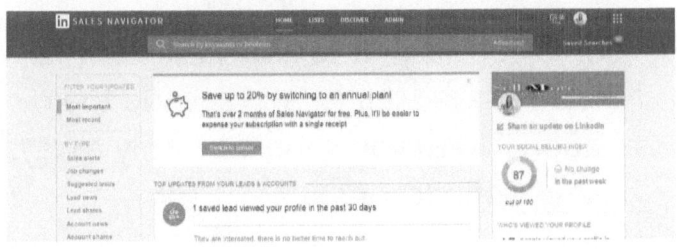

Step 3. Making connections with your target audience. On the top menu, click the

magnifying glass, don't type anything, and hit "search" - You will be taken to a blank search results page that looks a lot like this:

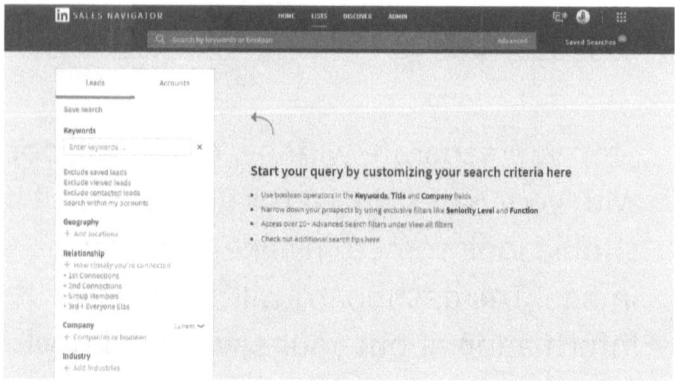

Step 4. My two rules for making connections is first to always select "Exclude saved leads" and second their relationship to you should be only always be 2nd Connections.

Excluding saved leads gets important on day two of this process.. It will save you a great deal of time in the long run so be sure to make this a habit.

We want to focus on second degree connections because those are people that you are more likely to actually already have some type of basis for a relationship. These are also people that you are more likely to actually bump into in real life which is really what this process is all about... networking digitally while you and your sales teams are out there doing it in-person.

Step 5. Use the filter options to create a segment of your 2nd degree connections that falls within your target audience. If you are unsure what filter settings are appropriate for your company, then please consult your friends at Mouth Marketing.

Step 6. Connect with anyone that you feel you have a strong reason to connect with such as a close connection or university affiliation.

Write a thoughtful, personalized message when sending an invitation to someone that you do not know personally. This is powerful more so now with the influx of bot-powered lead generating profiles. Stand out from the bots and really express an interest in the invitee.

Step 7. Do this every business day. Seriously. In the same way you set aside time for cold-calling, use this process.

Every person that you request to connect with will get an email in their inbox that includes your name, profile photo, and headline. This is the part of the process that makes your personal profile photo and headline super critical. If these aren't clear and professional, then your acceptance rates will often suffer.

Getting into a new everyday habit is a struggle for anybody, which is why it is important that leadership supports the sales and marketing teams and gets them excited about the results from the program. Change within the company procedures aren't always easy to roll out so I recommend stressing the commission opportunities and once they begin to catch fire, everyone will be on board. Most organizations start to see results within the first 30 days of consistent lead generation.

SOCIAL SELLING

Selling on social media has been done since the age of Myspace, but it hasn't always been done right. You have probably been exposed to oodles of bad examples so I am here to confirm your beliefs in that selling like a used car salesman on social media does not actually work.

Here are my recommendations for how to sell without blatantly selling on social media:

- + Share recent client success stories, but don't make it sound like a total testimonial. Share an update that says something like this: Had a fantastic call with a new client, they just shared that in their first month of applying my LinkedIn Lead Generation strategy they increased sales 50%!

- + Engage with your target audience on LinkedIn. Comment thoughtfully on their posts, comment as a human and not some weird selling robot. The goal is to build a real relationship. Like the things that they have to say if you like those things too and really follow your Sales

Navigator newsfeed for those pertinent updates.

+ Write articles that are native to LinkedIn. These articles can be less than 500 words and should be about relevant topics. If you have trouble with writer's block, then think about common problems that your clients and potential clients face... How are you solving those problems and what can someone do to try and remedy those issues?

+ Images... The people of LinkedIn and of social media everywhere love GOOD images and videos. Share photos of the teams, interesting shots around the office, photos from events, and if you decide to use stock images then make them powerful and relevant to what they are being used to represent.

- Native video posts on LinkedIn. In case you haven't seen the flood of videos in your feed, you now have the ability to upload video files directly to LinkedIn. I sometimes like to use video in place of simply writing a blog. Videos no longer than 3 minutes with captions are seeing the most success right now.

For leadership, I recommend providing your teams with questionnaires to inspire content creation on an ongoing basis. Creating a standard questionnaire really helps people think about creative ways to talk about what they do and who they are with their LinkedIn network. Things like, what is your favorite quote? Or, what is the best business advice that you've been given? Questions like these can inspire interesting and unique content, meanwhile maintaining that level of consistency.

How to Implement to Teams

Getting buy-in on content creation from the marketing department goes a lot like the daily connections discussion. In order for the daily connections to be worth anything, you need to nurture those leads within LinkedIn which requires some content creation. There are a few hacks to this that can save your teams some time, but custom created content really out-performs any canned content available.

What I recommend is really using the ramp-up period to get the most content out of your teams as possible. Make the lead generation announcement an exciting opportunity for them to see their commission checks significantly increase and ask them to get started by completing a questionnaire about themselves. Do you currently offer a commission bonus for your marketing team? Depending upon the size of your company and departmental objectives, this could be a way to incentivize the marketing team to get behind sales and strengthen their working relationship.

Questionnaires should be used to really get to know each person on the team not so much focus around the company and their role. Ask them to use complete sentences because the content they write may be used as conversation starters with potential clients on LinkedIn.

Content hack: For only $10 per month you can get access to the buffer.com content inbox which will create socially shareable content and links to relevant articles. All you have to do is go in and pick what content you want to be shared and they will automatically share it for you. There are different price points depending on the number of social accounts that you want to link to this, but it is totally worth it to sprinkle in some of these posts if you are creating your own content.

Please note that by using content inbox, you will be sharing posts with third-party links which LinkedIn does not prefer. Your content will attract more eyes in the newsfeed by sticking to native content and through encouraging your network to stay on LinkedIn.

How not to spam your network

It is super important that you, as a business leader understands that the data your sales and marketing teams have access to is incredibly valuable, but also regulated by various data and consumer protection laws.

LinkedIn gives connections the ability to view one anothers data such as your email address, phone numbers, addresses, Twitter handle, location, and more. This has led to some users abusing access to this level of information through creating ghost accounts actively requesting to connect with large quantities of people simply to harvest their data - dump - then do it all over again. This type of behavior has forced LinkedIn to reduce the amount of data access the users have which is why it is ultra critical that you develop your network and continuously download your data.

There are ways that you may use LinkedIn data without breaking CANSPAM, but as always - depending on your industry and objectives the rules may vary for you.

Ways to use LinkedIn data:

- Email retargeting campaigns

- Sending a personal email

- Making personal phone calls

- Adding to your CRM for tracking

What makes an email personal?

+ A personal email must have a clear "to" and "from" format.

+ The email must come from a personal email address such as ashley@mouthmarketingllc.com (do not use an info@mouthmarketingllc.com)

+ Do not ask for business in this email, but you may invite them to meet with you or discuss something with you.

I recommend that before allowing your sales or marketing teams to email anyone using their LinkedIn data to represent your business - for any reason - consult with your general counsel and ensure that you have collected this data appropriately for that specific use. Your general counsel will be familiar with this process and have likely helped guide other organizations on best practices around CANSPAM.

Maximum Impact

To really maximize the impact, you really want to follow through with the process. It seems so simple, but consistency is the biggest factor in reaching maximum impact. There are a few things that you can do to give you a leg up on the competition when it comes to this so here are a few things that you can do give you a boost:

+ Native video! < I mentioned this already, but LinkedIn algorithms favor native video posts. The more native video that you share, the more people will see it in their newsfeeds.

+ Avoid sharing articles that link to third-party websites. Again, LinkedIn algorithms do not want you to convince users to leave their site. They want native content.

+ Stay up to date on LinkedIn features. Become an early-adopter of their newest features and your account will be favored in the newsfeed.

+ Write articles about current events.

I recently shared an article on LinkedIn in regards to social selling specifically titled, "The Psychology Behind LinkedIn Lead Generation & Social Selling."

In the article, I wrote:

> By now you have probably received dozens of messages that are similar to the following:
>
>> Thanks for connecting on 12/22/2017, that alone has helped me. I would like to know whether to engage here or not. Please do reply so that I will stop emailing you if you're not interested. Whatever you decide and chose is perfectly fine. Lastly

> *please consider this short eBook and video I did on generating leads as a gift: http://www.sample-link.com that you can do on your own.*

Before I pick apart this message, I want to encourage you to pickup a copy of How to Win Friends & Influence People by Dale Carnegie. Honestly, you can read this book hundreds of times and learn new lessons, but the same methods outlined in this book may be applied to social selling and generating leads on LinkedIn.

In the above message (based off of a real message received), the recipient has no motivating reason to click that link. Why should we care? We have our own ways of generating leads, delete. This message may even come across as offensive to some recipients because not only do we not care about the content of the message, but it is spam!

So how then are people actually

generating leads through social selling?

They are addressing the why first. This is something that we talk about a lot in marketing, but many still fall short in actually achieving it let alone helping the sales team do the same.

Instead, we get what I refer to as "Stuart Spam" - Referring to Mad TV's Stuart skit from the 90s.

How do we avoid Stuart Spamming people? We acknowledge that our b2b recipients are people and people hate spam.

Here is an example of how the above message could be tweaked to establish a more meaningful relationship with the recipient:

> *Hi Ken,*
>
> *I know that we have been connected for some time on LinkedIn, but I don't believe that we have been formally*

> *introduced. I have been fascinated by your insightful posts and hope to learn more about you and your interesting work with Xcompany. Hope we can find time for a quick chat!*
>
> *Thank you,*
>
> *AJ*

Genuine interest in your network goes a long way in social selling. The world does not revolve around you and your business, quite frankly, people don't care until you give them a reason to and as Dale Carnegie said, "To be interesting, be interested."

I would also encourage you to consider that LinkedIn may not be a permanent marketing or sales solution. As many of us have come to understand, technology and communication platforms are ever-changing. We must always be adapting and taking what we know and applying it creatively to new platforms.

LinkedIn may not always offer these features as we know them in this book. LinkedIn may not always be around, but the lessons in motivating your team, social selling, automation, and tips may be used across platforms. How To Win Friends And Influence People was written nearly 100 years ago, but the lessons shared are still applicable today and this lesson is truly a reinforcement of those same principles.

What the future holds for LinkedIn users is unknown, but I hope to be a center for reason and suggestion to the platform. Writing recently, "Dear LinkedIn, A Letter From a Concerned User."

In it, I state my own concerns for the platform:

> *Dear LinkedIn,*
>
> *I have been an active user for many years now and have really built my business around the functionality and opportunities available because of LinkedIn. However, since the Microsoft takeover we have seen tremendous change and in ways that I do not feel will sustain long-term. We have lost features, gained "new" features, and now customer service is almost non-existent for the average user - I am*

writing this open letter because you have not taken the time to ask us - the user - how we feel. I could spend days going over in detail what I would change if LinkedIn were mine to run, but I will stick to just a few of my main concerns...

- *The roll-out of new services has been atrocious.*

The new features roll out process has been an issue for years, you have done an awful job at communicating these issues and updates. I have experienced this first-hand, as my profile is part of the last batch of accounts to have access to any newly released features (I didn't even have video capabilities until about three months ago, yet weeks prior you claimed everyone had it). I was given no explanation, other than some kind employee says "whoops, guess there are a few issues" - Let's also not forget last year when you changed the premium services functionalities.

Business premium is a hollow upgrade (for everyone else reading, don't waste your money on that just go straight for Sales Navigator) that when changed last year the users were given no warning other than some features suddenly disappeared.

- *The "new" features and other unoriginal ideas.*

I joke now when I speak about LinkedIn that if someone is ever curious as to what you are going to do next, then simply look at Facebook five years ago and there you have it... We now have location sharing information, we have video, we have ads on top of videos, we have the new and super annoying little chat boxes on the desktop version... I could go on, but it is really unoriginal and quite frankly, much more could be done to enhance the LinkedIn experience without trying to become more like Facebook (which I personally abhor). Here is a thought: What about compensating content creators that take the time to create valuable and thought-provoking content? Facebook doesn't do that and YouTube has been struggling to keep their content creators happy... That would be game-changing.

- *A shifting LinkedIn culture.*

Since many of these new features are in essence, Facebook features - We have started to see more "professionals" share completely inappropriate content on here which has ultimately resulted in a shift in the culture here. If 88% of your users are turning to the platform to get relevant industry news, then shouldn't the algorithms be doing their job better at giving the people what they want? Instead, we are starting to see that Facebook mentality of pushing the specific and sometimes controversial content higher in the newsfeed because it gets more engagement... even if it is negative engagement.

LinkedIn, I hope you understand that this isn't personal. I obviously still do a great deal of work promoting the platform, but help me help you build a better network.

Sincerely,

AJ - Ashley Johnson

LINKEDIN DATA

This changes every so often, but it is critical that you download your LinkedIn data at the very least once per month. As I mentioned, LinkedIn gives you access to a tremendous amount of valuable data on your connections. I want to stress again the importance that this data is not misused.

To begin tapping into the data that LinkedIn provides to you, I have compiled a few steps so you can capture your own below:

Step 1. Select "My Network" in the middle of the top menu of your LinkedIn account.

Step 2. Click "See all" in the section on the top left side of the page.

Step 3. Click "Manage synced and imported contacts" on the top left corner... almost looks like one of those weird text ads that nobody pays any attention to.

How To Generate Leads Using LinkedIn

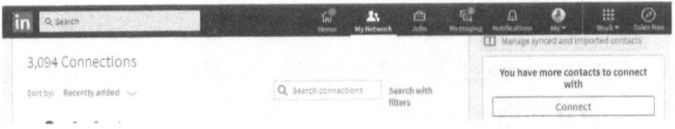

Step 4. Select "the works" and click "request archive" - A prompt will appear that requires you to re-enter your LinkedIn password. Be sure to enter your password and then select "request archive"

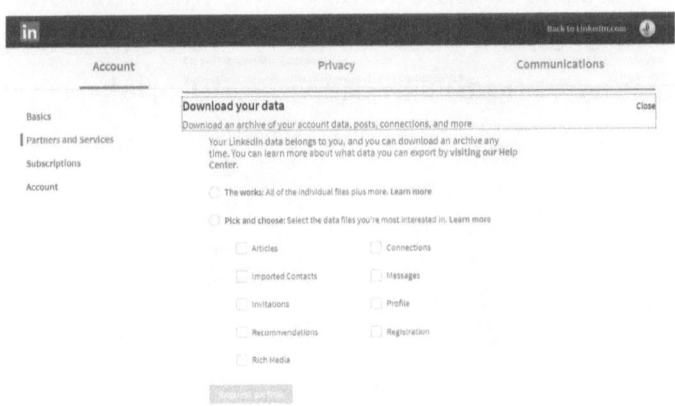

Once you have requested your archive, give LinkedIn about 15 minutes or so to compile the data. You will receive an email upon completion or you may simply refresh this page every 5-10 minutes to see if the file is ready to be downloaded.

Step 5. Once the file is ready, download the zip and extract the files. Within the zip file there is a spreadsheet labeled "connections" and this is where you will find information on each of your connections including: First name, last name, job title, company, email address, date connected on. *To upload this information into email marketing software, be sure to upload all of this information and label it appropriately - You can see how to do this in the video tutorial.

AUTOMATION

I am frequently asked about the many automation tools available to help make growing and nurturing your LinkedIn network much more efficient. This is a complicated topic, one that many legitimate LinkedIn lead generation specialists tend to avoid because many people tend to abuse the automated tools.

When is it okay to use automated tools? According to LinkedIn - never. Use these tools at your own risk, LinkedIn has deactivated accounts that have appeared to abuse the automated bot tools.

Who is most at risk getting caught using automated tools? Anyone that is caught doing things at an unusual rate, a sudden drastic change in platform behavior, spam or abuse complaints by other users, exceeding the outbound connection invitations limit.

What are automated LinkedIn tools like dux soup good for? This tool can be used to add custom tags to individual LinkedIn profiles, including notes allowing you to use LinkedIn almost like a CRM. The tool is great for endorsing skills for a small list of people that you want to stay top of mind with such as leads, colleagues, vendors, or clients.

There are many great video tutorials available by dux soup for pro subscribers, I highly recommend that if you decide to use this tool or any similar LinkedIn automation tools that you read about all of the risks and features before taking a test drive on your profile. Please also be sure to download your LinkedIn data prior and throughout the usage of these tools to ensure that should you lose access to your account, you still own your data.

If you are interested in using automated tools to simply give your hands a rest for a few minutes each day or to just simply maximize your time, then get *12-months of Dux Soup Pro 50%* off by visiting this link: https://jvz5.com/c/968695/166477

Dux Soup Merge Tag Tools

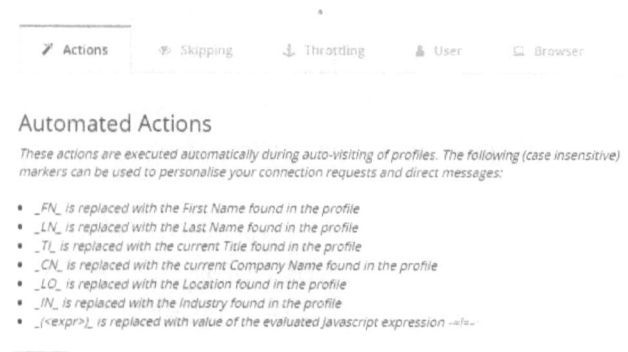

There are many reasons that Dux Soup is a really neat tool to use with LinkedIn, but these automated action tags are a huge time-saver. BUT - These can also get people in a lot of trouble. As you can see for an example, the merge tag _FN_ will automatically insert the first name wherever it is used within a message template.

Some people like to use Dux Soup to make outbound connection requests to people within their target audience, but it is important that you have a valid reason to connect with these people so make a compelling invitation message that might apply to a broader group and still make someone feel unique. That sounds complicated and that is because it is! Really put yourself in the shoes of the invitation recipient. Would you want to accept your invitation request based off of the message that you sent? Usually your first dozen message drafts are over-salesy so instead if you are using a bot to deliver outbound invitations be sure to set a search that is highly targeted and craft a message that applies uniquely to all recipients.

What Can Dux Soup Really Do?

OFF	Send connection requests to 2nd and 3rd degree connections during visits using standard LinkedIn or Sales Navigator.
OFF	Send a personalised message to 1st Degree Connections using standard LinkedIn or Sales Navigator
OFF	Send InMail™ to 2nd and 3rd degree connections during visits using Sales Navigator or Recruiter.
OFF	Follow any profile using Standard LinkedIn
OFF	Disconnect a profile from your network using Standard LinkedIn
OFF	Save any profile as 'Lead' using Sales Navigator
OFF	Save the profile as PDF file using Standard LinkedIn *(Disable confirmation of download location for each file via chrome://settings/downloads)*
OFF	Endorse [Top 3 ▼] skill(s) of a 1st degree connection using Standard LinkedIn
OFF	Tag profiles as [type your tag(s)] when auto-visiting *(Separate multiple tags with a comma, maximum of 5 tags)*
OFF	Run automated actions while manually browsing profiles

There are many useful Dux Soup options, but I recommend sticking to the safer tools that are less likely to raise any red flags if you choose to go this route.

My personal favorite tools are the Endorse Top 3 skills of a 1st degree connection using Standard LinkedIn and the Tag profiles as feature which makes keeping tabs on your leads much easier should you ever decide to do a drip messaging campaign using Dux Soup.

For example, if you want to send a message to your 1st degree network within your target audience, then anyone receiving that message should also be tagged as "message1" or something to indicate that they have received the first message in a series. This allows you to skip their profile in the future, which I will explain the importance of next.

Profile Skipping

Skipping profiles is critical in maintaining a clean campaign. I can't tell you how many times a "LinkedIn lead generation specialist" sends me the same crappy sales pitch message simply because they haven't organized or utilized appropriate profile tags.

Additionally, the profile skipping tab is a great way to reduce your odds of raising any red flags at LinkedIn.

My personal favorite skipping features:

- + Skipping if outside my network

- + Skipping if not a premium subscriber

- + Skipping if profile photo is blank

- + Skipping profiles tagged as

- + History skipper

I highly recommend always skipping people outside of your network. By turning that skip off, you can run into problems with LinkedIn because you will likely be reported as spam by other users.

Skipping anyone that isn't a premium subscriber is a great tool because premium users are more engaged in the platform and are more likely to connect and grow their network.

Users without profile photos are more

unlikely to accept invitation requests from people that they do not know personally, especially if you don't have a highly compelling reason to connect. It is best to skip these users as you may be more likely to be reported as spam resulting in account accessibility issues by LinkedIn. The skipping profiles tagged as and history skippers really come in handy for any lead nurturing and/or drip messaging campaigns managed natively within LinkedIn.

If you decide to use an automate tool such as dux soup, then know that you are using it solely at your own risk and LinkedIn does not allow the use of bots on their platform. Any "expert" pushing automated tools as a solution to your LinkedIn Lead Generation plan is often pushing overpriced garbage that will likely lead to your account being banned.

WILL IT WORK FOR YOU?

This particular LinkedIn lead generation strategy has been used by B2B sales and marketing teams of all sizes. This process has additionally been tested and proven in B2C settings such as event promotions, book sales, university recruitment and others.

They key to determining whether or not this strategy will be successful in meeting your objectives is through thorough planning and market research.

Below is a list of industries that have successfully used this strategy to develop and nurture leads:

- Legal Services
- Fundraising
- Marketing & Ad Agencies
- Web Development
- IT Services
- Telecommunications
- Benefits Brokerage Firms
- Mortgage Lenders
- Insurance Agencies
- Manufacturers
- Professional Coaches

- Media
- Authors
- Hospitality Vendors
- Commercial Service Providers
- Software & Technology
- Recruiting
- Commercial Real Estate
- Energy
- Photographers

There are countless ways that you can tweak this system to achieve your networking goals. You may use this system to generate sales leads, job search leads, or simply just to get in front of someone that you are intrigued by. The secret to success with this campaign is very much the same that can be applied to any marketing campaign or strategy - Clear planning and consistent follow through is critical to achieve success.

I encourage you to give more thought to the chapter on Motivating The Teams if you are attempting to encourage other people on your team or even employees to begin implementing this process. They need to fully understand why they are going to make this adjustment to their existing process.

Communicating the impact that the process can have on their personal objectives not just simply company. Your team will look like LinkedIn thought-leaders if they maintain this system effectively. As a leader, you need to recognize that your team is strong independently and with that comes power for them to leave. However, a successful salesperson doesn't quit - Give them the tools and incentives to stay. Motivate them to want it and encourage them to keep at it.

I recently shared an article on LinkedIn that I feel applies to not only this particular campaign, but may be applied to any role. The title, "Building a Profitable Marketing Team."

Here is what I shared:

> *With only 8% of brands being satisfied with their marketing agency partners, that leaves many considering the development of an in-house marketing*

agency. There are many reasons why moving operations internally can benefit your organization, but without the proper know-how it can come at a higher cost. Building an internal marketing team starts at the hiring process, but is defined during the training process and many companies with limited departmental-specific leadership can often fail to provide enough training and education. This is a scary realization when you read research that shows a full 40% of employees who don't receive the necessary job training to become effective will leave their positions within the first year. Even worse, the typical cost to replace an employee can be 1.5-2x their annual salary!

You need more direct attention than your agency partner is capable of providing within your budget, but you don't have the technical skills to answer your entry-level marketer's questions. What can you do?

Hiring an experienced senior marketer full-time can often be financially out of reach for many companies, but by hiring a properly trained entry-level marketer to manage smaller projects internally the company can reduce cost and/or save time. In fact, according to the Association for Talent Development (ATD), companies that offer comprehensive training programs have 218% higher income per employee than companies without formalized training. But it doesn't stop there. These companies also enjoy a 24% higher profit margin than those who spend less on training.

The numbers don't lie, ensure that your team gets the proper training and development. Hire an experienced independent Marketing Consultant to train and develop your growing internal marketing team you can reduce cost and increase revenue.

After considering those numbers, it may be worth considering holding off on your first internal marketing hire until you are able to find a suitable consultant or fractional marketing leader to train them.

What other reasons might you considering hiring fractional or consulting-basis help to support your marketing objectives? There are many reasons to consider hiring a consultant to optimize your processes and strategies. As an entrepreneur myself, I have had to hire consultants to advise me on my growing business. If anything, for the outside perspective because it is so easy to be bogged down in the day to day of the business that we often forget to finish the supporting projects that we need to complete in order to sustain growth.

Even if something is your own specialty, you might consider hiring an independent consultant to bounce ideas off of you. For example: I advise other marketing agencies on LinkedIn because that is one of my niche specialities whereas they often are very comfortable using LinkedIn, but they might have specific lead generation or platform questions that I can quickly answer for them.

Often entrepreneurs and executives can

find that their existing sales and marketing strategies are not delivering the results that had anticipated or maybe even once used to achieve. This could be the result of a changing market or perhaps communication preferences have changed and your demographics research is dated. Whatever the case may be, an independent consultant may be a good person to have analyzing your opportunities and recommending solutions to overcome any new barriers that may have popped up in your market space.

AJ - Ashley Johnson

ABOUT THE AUTHOR

AJ, born Ashley Taylor Johnson has been focused on innovating the marketing and advertising industry. In 2015, she founded Mouth Marketing - a lead generation and startup marketing firm. Prior to the launch of the agency, AJ worked in an array of digital marketing and marketing consulting roles. She has advised private, public, and nonprofit organizations on projects ranging from market positioning to comprehensive communications strategies.

AJ - Ashley Johnson

AJ first discovered her passion for entrepreneurship and social media marketing while still in high school where she taught herself how to develop unique Myspace page designs. Eventually her designs caught the attention of friends and local artists that were interested in commissioning her work. While studying Marketing and Public Relations at Indiana University Northwest, AJ was simultaneously discovering new ways to market on social media and began consulting local businesses on Myspace, Twitter, Facebook, and Foursquare.

Today, AJ is passionate about helping organizations boost profit margins through strategic marketing consulting and acting as Director of Marketing to successfully train and build sustainable internal marketing teams that can successfully translate executive objectives into marketing strategy. She works with companies to improve profit margins by at least 24% through structured employee training and strategic marketing consulting.

Areas that AJ provides specialized training and support for client employees: Email Marketing, Social Media Marketing, Wordpress Management, SEO, Content Marketing, PPC, Photoshop, CRM Management, Marketing Analytics, Traditional Marketing, Digital Marketing, Marketing Technology, Marketing Management, Marketing Operations, Tradeshow Coordination, Marketing Automation, Product Marketing, Market Research, Branding, Product Branding, Marketing Logistics, Lean Marketing, Lead Generation, LinkedIn Marketing, B2B Marketing, B2C Marketing, Strategic Planning, Departmental Human Resources, Marketing Recruitment Consulting.

Industries she has worked with: Finance, Logistics & Transportation, Medical Technology, Energy & Renewables, Media & Broadcast, Marketing & Advertising, Telehealth, Commercial & Residential Construction, Manufacturing, Professional Services, Insurance & Benefits, Software &

Technology, Telecommunications, Hospitality, Non-profits, Residential & Commercial Real Estate, Distribution, and more.

Would you like to keep in touch?

Connect with AJ on LinkedIn:
www.linkedin.com/in/ashleymarketing/

@AJonLinkedIn

Keep an eye out for my next LinkedIn book, "How To Land *The* Job Using LinkedIn"

www.ingramcontent.com/pod-product-compliance
Lightning Source LLC
Chambersburg PA
CBHW031444210526
45464CB00005B/2320